Your Life in COMICS

100 Things for Guys to Write and Draw

created by Bill Zimmerman, artwork by Tyler Page

free spirit
PUBLISHING®

THIS BOOK BELONGS TO:

Alexander Vinas

DATE BEGUN:

2013

Library of Congress Cataloging-in-Publication Data
Zimmerman, William, 1941-
 Your life in comics : 100 things for guys to write and draw / created by Bill Zimmerman ; artwork by Tyler Page.
   p. cm.
 ISBN 978-1-57542-351-7
 1. Boys—Social life and customs—Juvenile literature. 2. Boys—Comic books, strips, etc.—Juvenile literature. 3. Comic books and children—Juvenile literature. 4. Comic books, strips, etc.—Social aspects—Juvenile literature. I. Page, Tyler, 1976- II. Title.
 HQ784.C6Z56 2010
 741.5'1083—dc22

                                                                        010014592

Reading Level Grades 3–4; Interest Level Ages 9–13;
Fountas & Pinnell Guided Reading Level P

Edited by Douglas J. Fehlen
Cover and interior design by Tasha Kenyon

10 9 8 7 6 5 4 3 2 1
Printed in the United States of America
U19810710

Free Spirit Publishing Inc.
217 Fifth Avenue North, Suite 200
Minneapolis, MN 55401-1299
(612) 338-2068
help4kids@freespirit.com
www.freespirit.com

Dear Reader,

You know how most other books give you all the words and illustrations so you don't have a say about what happens? Well, this book isn't like that. Instead, it's a do-it-yourself comic book where you can tell stories from your life. There are also cartoons where you get to decide what happens to other characters—just follow the prompts and fill in the **talk** and **thought** balloons to determine what the people say and think. Their fate is in your hands! You'll also find pages where you can draw comic strips of your own.

What kind of stuff will you write about and draw in this book? It's up to you. Some of the pages are funny and some are serious. Many are about family, friends, or other people you know. A lot are about things you may have experienced in your life, others probably not. (Unless maybe you *have* met space aliens or done some time traveling). One quality all the pages share is that they are incomplete. They need your imagination to be finished. All you need is something to write with and your good ideas.

Time to enjoy yourself. Have fun!

Sincerely,

Bill Zimmerman

P.S. For more fun, visit my website (www.makebeliefscomix.com). There you can create comic strips and share cartoon ideas of your own. You can also visit www.freespirit.com/comics for downloadable activities and website extensions from this book.

Before You Get Started . . .

Many of the activities in this book let you fill in talk and thought balloons to complete comics. You'll also have the chance to draw comics of your own. Whenever you see this logo [logo] start drawing.

If you don't think you can create the kind of detailed drawings you might see in some comic books, don't worry. Creating comics is all about finding the style that's right for you. You can make really complex drawings to tell your stories if you want, but simple illustrations are okay, too.

Like this guy, who we'll call Mister Mustache, and his dog, Buster:

Once you have your first scene, the next step is pretty simple . . . just make something happen. It can be anything you want. Like maybe Mister Mustache and Buster walk by a squirrel eating nuts in the park. What do you think will happen next?

That's all it takes. Once you begin a comic strip, you can make it go wherever you like. If you're lucky, your story might even take on a life of its own.

Disclaimer: Your comic strip stories can be a lot less corny than this one! Remember, just use your imagination!

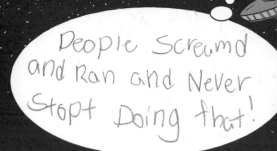

People screamd and Ran and Never Stopt Doing that!

THEN . . . the Aliens went Bak Hom to ther Hom and came Bak the Next Day even in high school But ther were tird and Fustrated Becoas people saind Stop ?

AFTER THAT . . .

FINALLY . . .

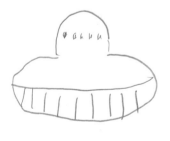

Interested in real efforts to track down life in space? Visit the **NASA** website (www.nasa.gov) to find updates on the International Space Station, Hubble Space Telescope, Mars orbiter, and other projects helping us learn more about the universe.

MY HAPPIEST MEMORY IS . . . .

Geting to Kiss my GrilFreind all the time in School inthe School Bath Room Wen No Won Was Looking at us

Hollywood is making a movie about your life.

1) What's it called? team Beach

2) Who's playing you? A Gril anSome Boys

3) Is it a comedy, adventure, drama, or something else? NO But it is a song and movie

4) What's the storyline? Yes yes yes you Got that right

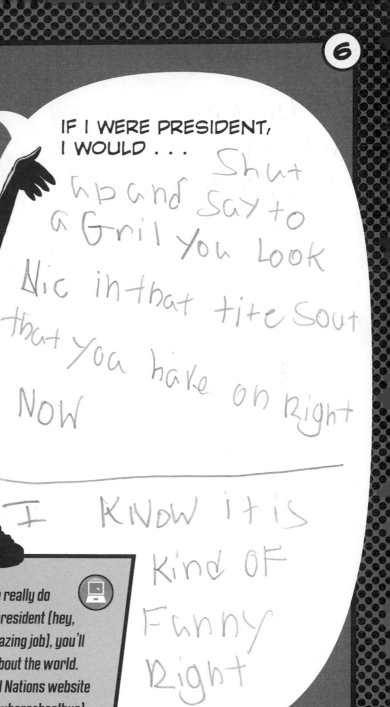

IF I WERE PRESIDENT, I WOULD . . .

Shut up and say to a Gril you Look Nic in that tite sout that you have on Right NOW

_____

I KNOW it is Kind OF Funny Right

If your plans in life really do include becoming president (hey, you might do an amazing job), you'll need to know a lot about the world. Check out this United Nations website (www.un.org/pubs/cyberschoolbus). It has all kinds of info on each member country and the biggest challenges our planet faces.

I LOVE TO . . . Play and Galp Food in my mouth Like all way s YouRNOW Right the Day BeFor that even happen i the

Hous

Top 3 Most Important Things in My Life

1) Tak car of my mothe and talk Car all times

2) thing i can Do in school

3) DO MY home Wark

Design your own website.

Like what you see? Make a website of your own at a blog hosting site. A few popular (and free) sites are WordPress (www.wordpress.org), Blogger (www.blogger.com), and Blogsome (www.blogsome.com). These sites take you through step-by-step directions for creating fun websites. You can also create your own profile page at an online community (see #75 for some options).

Write a text message to a friend.

Draw a CD cover for an album you and your band have recorded.

Two best friends invent a cool new greeting.

A Day on Girl Planet

You're working on a scientific discovery that will change the world. Draw and explain your idea.

a valcaivo is eRupting

Did you know that when a dolphin or whale sleeps, half of its brain shuts down while the other half is active? Because these water mammals must rise to the surface of the ocean to breathe, they cannot completely go unconscious or would risk dying. Visit Science News for Kids (www.sciencenewsforkids.org) for all kinds of interesting facts about our planet.

Ghost Story

GUY COMIX

THE NEXT MORNING . . .

What are they talking about?

THE CRAZIEST THING I EVER DID WAS . . .

You can be any person from history . . .

1) Who would you be?

2) Why?

3) How would you change history?

Want to brush up on your knowledge of famous figures from history? Learn about heroes and tyrants from the near and distant past at Kidipede (www.historyforkids.org).

Skywriting (fill the sky with words)

Top 3 Superpowers You Want

1) ....

2) ....

3) ....

Take your superpowers and create your superhero physique. It's no sweat at the website of Marvel Comics (www.marvel.com/create_your_own_superhero), where you can morph yourself into a lean, mean, evil-fighting machine.

26 **Draw yourself playing with your favorite sports or music star. (Or add your photos together in a collage.)**

You have an idea for a new reality TV show.

1) What's it called? _____

2) What happens? _____
_____
_____
_____

Who is your best friend and why?

A Trip in a Time Machine

HIS ARRIVAL

HE MEETS SOMEONE OR SOMETHING

TO STAY OR RETURN HOME?

Technology Shutdown!

How will you survive three days without your electronic gadgets?

FIRST DAY

SECOND DAY

THIRD DAY

What's the plan?

AT SCHOOL . . .

AT HOME . . .

WITH FRIENDS . . .

Draw an Embarrassing Moment

Top 5 Fun Things to Do

1)

2)

3)

4)

5)

MY BIGGEST ACHIEVEMENT SO FAR HAS BEEN . . .

Accomplishing your goals can take a lot of hard work. Sometimes it's nice to have a little help along the way. The Boys and Girls Clubs of America (www.bgca.org) and Big Brothers Big Sisters of America (www.bbbs.org) connect teens with adult mentors.

COOL!

AT SCHOOL . . .

AT HOME . . .

WITH FRIENDS . . .

INVISIBLE GUY REVEALED

You've received a very important letter.

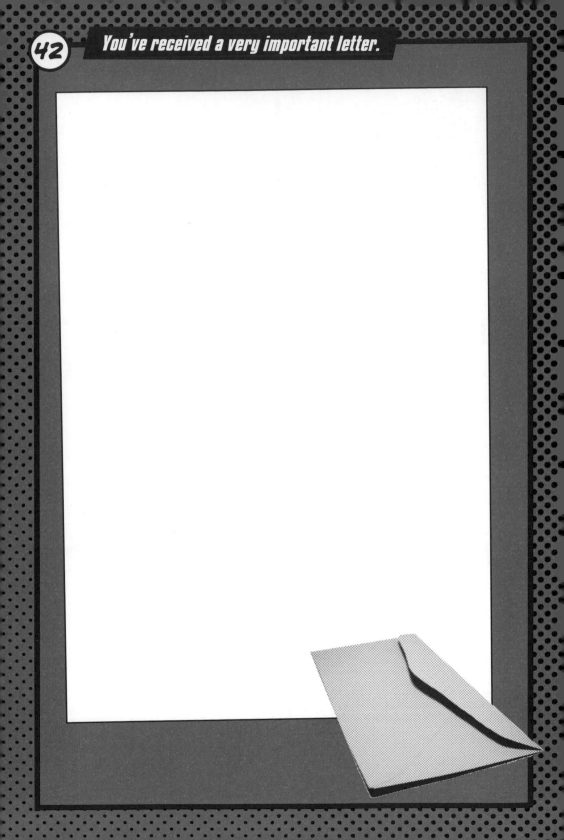

Cave Drawings

Write something in a secret language that no one but you can figure out.

Write the translation upside down just in case you forget the secret code. Or write everything backward so the only way to read your writing is by holding it up to the mirror.

Are you really into codes? Go online and check out the Cryptoclub (www.cryptoclub.math.uic.edu) to create all different kinds of codes. Programs can help you break down codes containing any letters and numbers. There are also jokes and games that let you put your code-cracking skills into action.

Mr. Popular

I'M SORRY ABOUT . . .

47

Words for a new song you are writing.

Title: _____

_____

Lyrics: _____

_____

_____

_____

_____

_____

_____

_____

_____

_____

_____

A First Date Where Everything Went Wrong

AT THE COFFEE SHOP . . .

A First Date Where Everything Went Right

AT THE COFFEE SHOP . . .

AT THE MOVIES . . .

SAYING GOOD-BYE . . .

AT THE MOVIES . . .

SAYING GOOD-BYE . . .

49 **No one knows this about me:**

You can write this in your secret code or language (see #45).

Who's your hero and why?

(Add a photo or draw the person if you like.)

Heroes are everywhere. The My Hero Project (www.myhero.com) has stories about people from all over the world who have accomplished extraordinary things. Visit the site to learn more about famous and everyday heroes who are changing the world one person at a time.

On the billboard, write a message to the world.

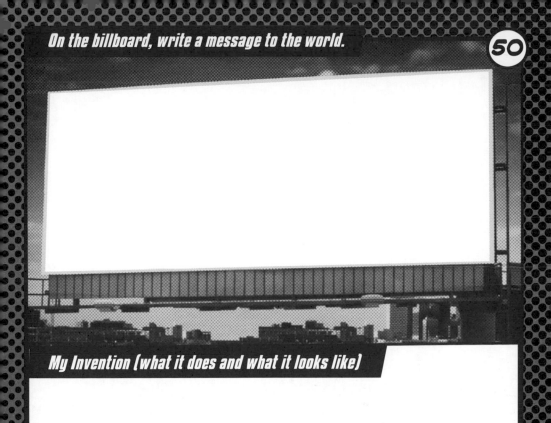

My Invention (what it does and what it looks like)

Do you have a lot of interest in gadgets? Visit How Stuff Works (www.howstuffworks.com) for the secrets behind how computers, machines, and all kinds of other things function.

BREAKFAST

GOING OUT TOGETHER

HANGING OUT AT HOME

53

Design a new kind of school locker and decorate it.

Write the story of your life in no more than 140 characters.

Mastered telling your life story in 140 characters or less? Think you could do it in six words? Log on to www.smithteens.com to learn more about six-word memoirs, a national project in which teens sum up their lives in half a dozen words.

THE MOST IMPORTANT
THING I KNOW IS . . .

What place would you like to visit? Why?

Where? _____

_____

Why? _____

_____

_____

_____

_____

A canvas awaits your sketch.

Top 5 Favorite Websites

1) _____

2) _____

3) _____

4) _____

5) _____

THE ONE THING THAT
DRIVES ME CRAZY IS . . .

It's your high school reunion 25 years from now, and you are a big success. What have you achieved?

Have a goal you'd like to reach? Sometimes another person helping can make all the difference in the world. Mentor (www.mentor.org) is an organization that connects teens with adults who can share knowledge about different careers or interest areas.

An Unexpected Adventure

GUY COMIX

S
U
D
D
E
N
L
Y
.
.
.

THEN . . .

FINALLY . . .

He's thinking about his goal.

You have discovered a new star in the universe. Name and draw it.

Top 3 Things You Want to Do in Your Life

1)

2)

3)

You can live in your favorite book . . .

1) What book did you choose?

2) Which character are you?

3) How does the story change now that you're in it?

Do you have a hard time finding books that are right for you? A lot of guys have this problem. That's why one famous author, Jon Scieszka, created a website called GuysRead (www.guysread.com). You can log on for some great reading recommendations and links to the websites of your favorite authors.

The Day Everything Went Wrong

AT SCHOOL . . .

The Day Everything Went Right

AT SCHOOL . . .

AT HOME . . .

WITH YOUR FRIENDS . . .

AT HOME . . .

WITH YOUR FRIENDS . . .

A TIME WHEN SOMEONE HELPED ME WAS . . .

Create a Mission Impossible for your best friend.

A Knock-Knock Joke

Top 3 Accomplishments You're Proud Of

1)

2)

3)

Create an avatar to represent you on the Web.

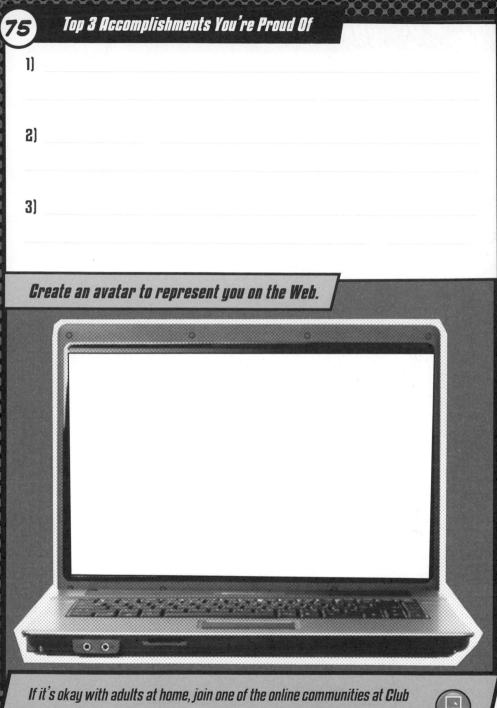

If it's okay with adults at home, join one of the online communities at Club Penguin (www.clubpenguin.com), Whyville (whyville.net), or Nicktropolis (nicktropolis.com). These virtual worlds allow you to create your own character and environments not to mention hang out with your friends.

A Grandfather's Good Words

What's on their minds?

YOUR EARLIEST MEMORY

MEETING YOUR BEST FRIEND

A HUGE ACCOMPLISHMENT

ANOTHER HIGHLIGHT

You've created a new extreme sport.

1) What's it called? _____

2) How do you do it? _____

_____

3) How do you win? _____

_____

Design a robot to make your life easier.

Okay, say you wanted to build this robot or another cool invention that will change the world. What could you do? One option: Visit the BKFK website (www.bkfk.com), a place where you can find inventing tips and enter inventions in contests. (Winners' ideas are made into products!) There are also profiles of other young people and their innovations to get you inspired.

He's thinking about his biggest challenge.

Some Good Advice

A Promise You Have Made to Yourself

Draw the best bedroom of all time.

Plan for the Perfect Birthday

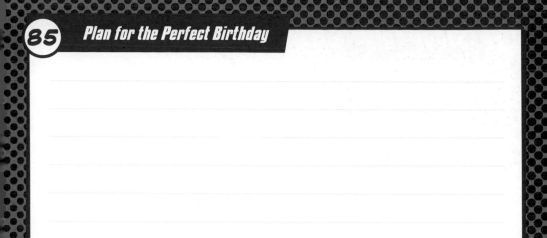

The Ultimate Menu

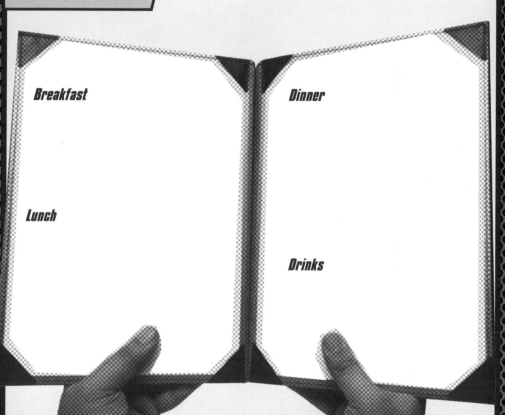

Breakfast

Dinner

Lunch

Drinks

Have questions about food, fitness, friendship, life? Visit the BAM! site (www.bam.gov) for fun games and interesting information about all kinds of stuff that matters. There's also expert advice on topics like puberty and getting along with others.

Slope Talk

Skate Boy's Best Tricks

Want to learn some wild moves of your own? Get a deck up by visiting Skateboard Science at Exploratorium (www.exploratorium.edu/skateboarding). Here you'll find the science behind skateboarding tricks and how you can perform them.

Print a copy of this page at www.freespirit.com/comics

An Important Conversation

In the morning . . .

A Proud Moment

GUY COMIX

TRANSPORTATION IN THE YEAR 2040

NEW SUPERHERO IN THE YEAR 2050

NEW INVENTION IN THE YEAR 2075

ANOTHER PREDICTION

Real Life Heroics

What's he angry about?

Your luckiest day (what happened?)

Whispers

He's giving himself a pep talk.

You in the Future

IN HIGH SCHOOL

HANGING WITH FRIENDS

AT YOUR JOB

WITH YOUR FAMILY

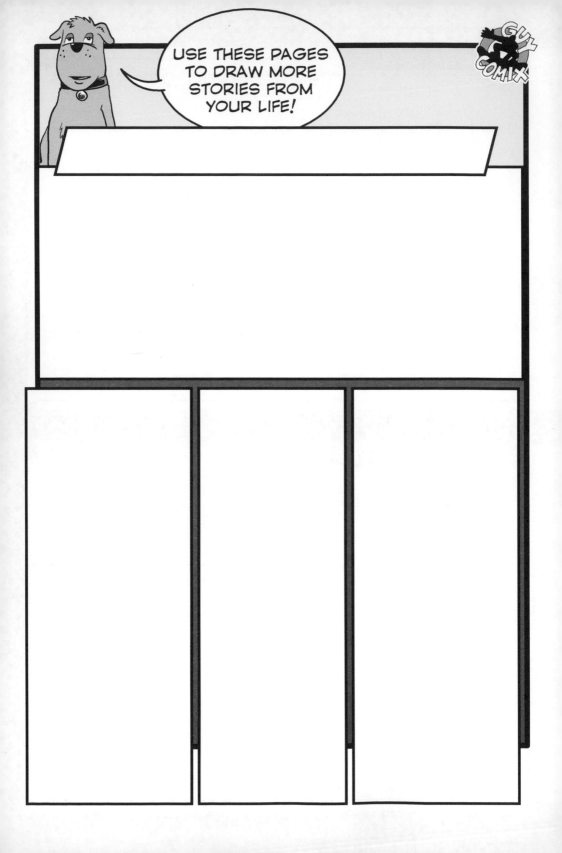

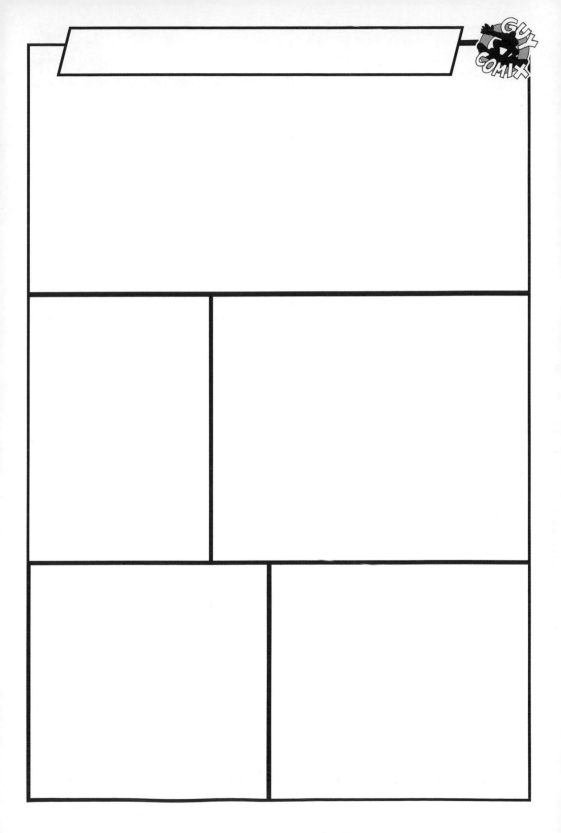

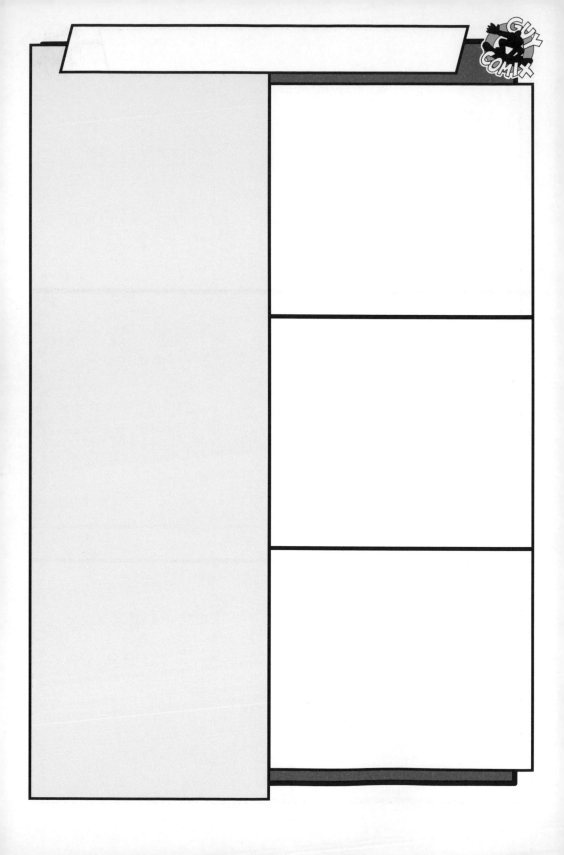

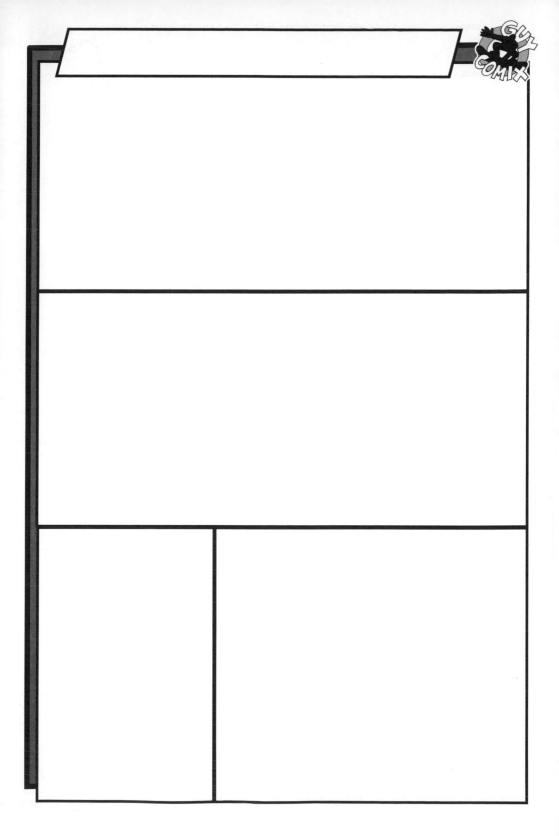

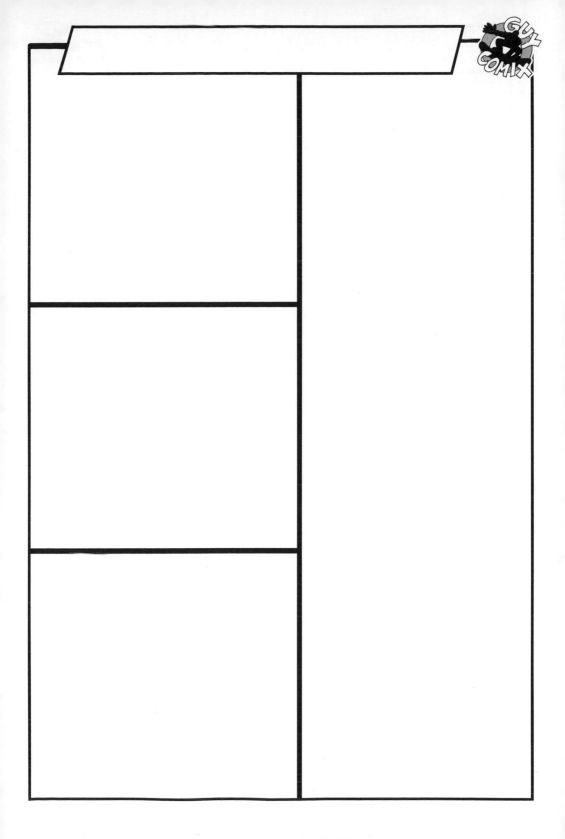

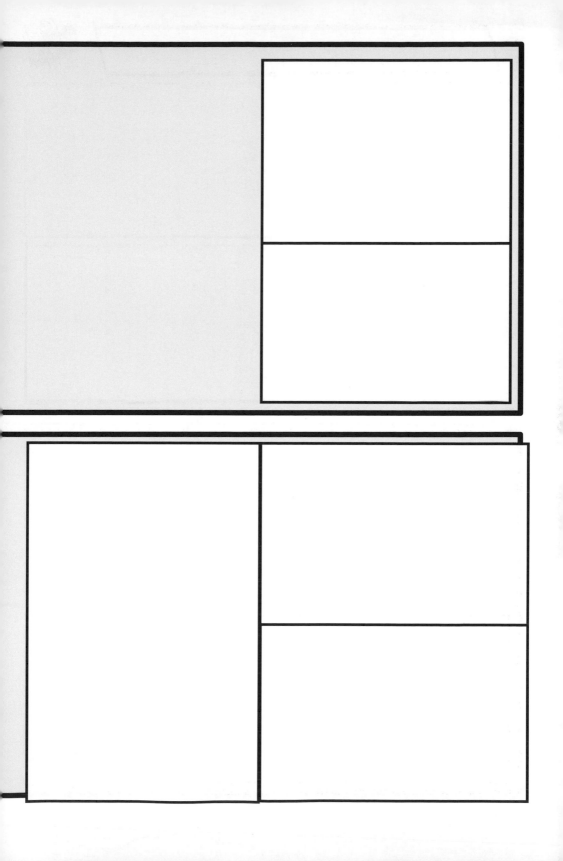

A Note from the Author

Ever since I was a boy, I've loved comics because they're so simple. They don't require long paragraphs to tell a story. Instead, only a few words are needed for the characters to share their lives. I hope you've enjoyed using comic strips to tell stories from your life.

Now that you've finished, I'd like to learn about any ideas you have for creating comics. It's possible I will work on another book like this in the future, and your comic strip ideas might be a perfect fit. When you send ideas, include your name and address along with parent permission to use your suggestions. If I am able to use one of your ideas in a future book, you will get a free copy.

Send ideas for comic strips or other activities to:

Bill Zimmerman
c/o Free Spirit Publishing
217 Fifth Avenue North, Suite 200
Minneapolis, MN 55401-1299
help4kids@freespirit.com

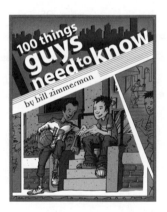

P.S. If you liked *Your Life in Comics,* you might also enjoy reading my book *100 Things Guys Need to Know* (available at www.freespirit.com). It's full of comic strips and other cool things about being a guy.

This book is dedicated to my dad, who used to bring home the Sunday comics each week and who bought me my first comic book. With thanks to my editor, Douglas Fehlen, for all his encouragement and great help in finding the websites cited throughout this book. —B.Z.